Updated Cambodia Travel Guide

Emily Michaels

Updated Cambodia Travel Guide

Updated Cambodia Travel Guide

A Comprehensive Guide to Explore the Rich History, iconic tourist spots, Natural Wonders, Vibrant Culture, and Stunning Landscapes of Cambodia and Travel Tips from Locals

By

Emily Michaels

Copyright © **Emily Michaels** [2023]

All rights reserved. No part of this book may be reproduced, stored in a retrieval system, or transmitted in any form or by any means, electronic, mechanical, photocopying, recording, or otherwise, without the prior written permission of the copyright owner.

Disclaimer:

The information provided in this book, "Updated Cambodia Travel Guide," is for general informational purposes only. While I have made every effort to ensure the accuracy and timeliness of the information, I do not make any representations or warranties of any kind, express or implied, about the completeness, accuracy, reliability, suitability, or availability of the information contained in this guide. Any reliance you place on such information is strictly at your own risk.

The book serves as a guide and should not substitute professional advice or serve as a guarantee of the conditions, safety, or quality of the destinations, accommodations, services, or activities mentioned. I disclaim any liability for any loss, injury, or inconvenience sustained by any reader as a result of the information or advice presented in this book.

It is recommended that readers independently verify and confirm any important information, such as visa requirements, health and safety guidelines, and local laws and regulations,

Updated Cambodia Travel Guide

before traveling to Cambodia. The author shall not be held liable for any inaccuracies or changes in the information provided.

Updated Cambodia Travel Guide

Updated Cambodia Travel Guide

Updated Cambodia Travel Guide

Table of content

Table of content 8
Introduction 11
    Why Visit Cambodia 14
    Quick Facts about Cambodia 17
    How To Use This Guide 19
Planning Your Trip 21
    Best Time to Visit 23
    Visa Requirements 25
    Currency and Exchange Rates 27
    Health and Safety Tips 30
    Transportation Options 33
Exploring Phnom Penh 37
    Top Attractions 39
    Dining and Nightlife 41
    Shopping Experiences 44
    Accommodation Options 47
Siem Reap and Angkor Wat 49
    Exploring the Angkor Archaeological Park 51
    Other Attractions in Siem Reap 56
    Local Cuisine and Dining Recommendations 59
    Accommodation Options 61
Coastal and Island Getaways 63

Updated Cambodia Travel Guide

    Sihanoukville 65

    Koh Rong and Koh Rong Samloem 67

    Kep and Kampot 69

    Beach Activities and Water Sports 71

Exploring the Countryside 73

    Battambang 75

    Kampong Cham 77

    Kratie and the Irrawaddy Dolphins 79

    Mondulkiri and Ratanakiri 81

    Eco-Tourism and Nature Reserves 83

Practical Information 85

    Essential Travel Resources 86

    Communication and Internet Access 89

    Local Customs and Etiquette 91

    Safety Tips and Emergency Contacts 93

Conclusion 97

Updated Cambodia Travel Guide

Updated Cambodia Travel Guide

Introduction

Located in Southeast Asia, Cambodia is a captivating country known for its rich history, magnificent temples, vibrant culture, and warm hospitality. Nestled between Thailand, Laos, and Vietnam, Cambodia offers a unique blend of ancient wonders, bustling cities, serene landscapes, and an emerging modernity. From the awe-inspiring temples of Angkor Wat to the charming streets of Phnom Penh, Cambodia invites travelers to immerse themselves in a world of captivating experiences.

Cambodia's history stretches back centuries, leaving behind a legacy that has shaped the country's identity. From the powerful Khmer Empire to the French colonial era and the tragic period of the Khmer Rouge, Cambodia's past has both inspired and challenged its people. Today, the nation stands as a testament to resilience and progress, inviting visitors to explore its historical sites, learn from its past, and appreciate its present.

One of the main highlights of Cambodia is undoubtedly the Angkor Archaeological Park, a UNESCO World Heritage Site. The park encompasses the legendary temples of Angkor, including the iconic Angkor Wat, the largest religious monument in the world. These magnificent structures, adorned with intricate carvings and surrounded by lush jungles, are a testament to the architectural genius of the Khmer civilization. Exploring the temples at sunrise or sunset offers a truly magical experience, transporting visitors to a bygone era.

Beyond the ancient wonders of Angkor, Cambodia's capital city, Phnom Penh, beckons with its own allure. A bustling metropolis with a vibrant street life, Phnom Penh offers a blend of traditional and modern attractions. Visitors can delve into the country's recent history at the somber Tuol Sleng Genocide Museum and the Killing Fields, gaining insight into the Khmer Rouge regime and paying tribute to the victims. The Royal Palace and Silver Pagoda showcase Cambodia's rich royal heritage, while the lively markets, riverside promenades, and culinary delights offer a taste of everyday life in the capital.

Beyond the major cities, Cambodia's countryside reveals a different facet of the country. From the serene beauty of the Tonle Sap Lake, Southeast Asia's largest freshwater lake, to the picturesque landscapes of Battambang and the rustic charms of rural villages, Cambodia's countryside offers a chance to experience a more laid-back and authentic way of life. Exploring the coastal regions of Sihanoukville, Kep, and Kampot allows visitors to unwind on pristine beaches, indulge in fresh seafood, and explore charming colonial architecture.

Cambodia's cultural heritage is also deeply ingrained in its performing arts, traditional crafts, and religious practices. Visitors can witness mesmerizing Apsara dance performances,

Updated Cambodia Travel Guide

partake in local festivals such as Bon Om Touk (Water Festival) or Khmer New Year, and visit local artisans to witness the creation of intricate silk textiles and handicrafts.

With its unique blend of history, culture, and natural beauty, Cambodia offers a truly enriching and unforgettable travel experience. This updated Cambodia Travel Guide aims to provide comprehensive information, insider tips, and practical advice to help travelers make the most of their journey, navigate the country with ease, and uncover the hidden gems that make Cambodia a remarkable destination.

Why Visit Cambodia

Cambodia is a country that captivates the hearts and imaginations of travelers from around the world. From its awe-inspiring ancient temples to its vibrant culture and stunning natural landscapes, Cambodia offers a plethora of reasons to make it your next travel destination. Here are some compelling reasons why you should visit Cambodia:

1. **Ancient Temples:** The magnificent temples of Angkor Wat and the Angkor Archaeological Park are undoubtedly the crown jewels of Cambodia. Exploring these UNESCO World Heritage sites allows you to witness the grandeur of the Khmer Empire and marvel at the intricate architectural details that have stood the test of time.
2. **Rich History:** Cambodia's history is both fascinating and poignant. From the rise and fall of the Khmer Empire to the dark period of the Khmer Rouge regime, Cambodia's past is deeply woven into its identity. By visiting historical sites like the Killing Fields and the Tuol Sleng Genocide Museum, you can gain a deeper understanding of the country's complex history and pay tribute to its resilience.
3. **Warm Hospitality:** Cambodians are known for their warm and welcoming nature. Whether you're exploring bustling markets or visiting rural villages, you'll be greeted with genuine smiles and kindness. Interacting with the locals provides an opportunity to

learn about their traditions, taste authentic cuisine, and forge connections that can last a lifetime.

4. **Natural Beauty:** Beyond the temples, Cambodia boasts stunning natural landscapes. From the tranquil beaches of Sihanoukville and the idyllic islands of Koh Rong to the lush jungles of Mondulkiri and the scenic countryside of Kampot, the country offers diverse and breathtaking scenery that appeals to nature lovers and adventure enthusiasts alike.

5. **Vibrant Culture:** Cambodia's vibrant culture is evident in its traditional arts, dance, and music. Witnessing a traditional Apsara dance performance or attending local festivals provides a glimpse into the country's rich cultural heritage. Exploring local markets, sampling street food, and interacting with artisans allow you to immerse yourself in the daily rhythms of Cambodian life.

6. **Affordable Travel:** Cambodia is known for its affordability, making it an attractive destination for budget-conscious travelers. Accommodation, transportation, and food options cater to a range of budgets, allowing you to experience the country's wonders without breaking the bank.

7. **Responsible Tourism:** By visiting Cambodia, you have the opportunity to support responsible tourism initiatives that benefit local communities and preserve the country's natural and cultural heritage. Engaging in activities like volunteering, supporting social enterprises, or opting for eco-friendly accommodations contributes to sustainable development.

Cambodia offers a unique blend of history, culture, and natural beauty that leaves a lasting impression on all who visit. Whether you're seeking ancient wonders, cultural immersion, or simply a memorable adventure, Cambodia promises an unforgettable experience that will leave you yearning to return.

Quick Facts about Cambodia

1) Cambodia is located in Southeast Asia and is bordered by Thailand, Laos, and Vietnam.
2) The official name of the country is the Kingdom of Cambodia.
3) The capital city of Cambodia is Phnom Penh.
4) The official language is Khmer, but English is widely spoken in urban areas and tourist destinations.
5) Cambodia has a population of over 16 million people.
6) The currency of Cambodia is the Cambodian Riel (KHR), but US dollars are widely accepted.
7) The country has a tropical climate with a wet season from May to October and a dry season from November to April.
8) Angkor Wat, a UNESCO World Heritage site, is Cambodia's most famous landmark and a major tourist attraction.
9) The temple complex of Angkor Wat was built in the 12th century and is the largest religious monument in the world.
10) Buddhism is the predominant religion in Cambodia, practiced by over 95% of the population.
11) Cambodian cuisine is known for its unique flavors and includes dishes like Amok, a traditional curry, and Nom Banh Chok, rice noodles with fish curry.
12) The Khmer Rouge regime led by Pol Pot was responsible for a genocide that occurred between 1975

and 1979, resulting in the deaths of an estimated 1.7 million people.
13) The Tonle Sap Lake is the largest freshwater lake in Southeast Asia and home to floating villages and diverse wildlife.
14) Cambodia has several national parks and protected areas, including the Cardamom Mountains and the Preah Vihear Temple.
15) The Cambodian flag consists of three horizontal stripes of blue, red, and blue, with a depiction of the Angkor Wat temple in the center.
16) Cambodian traditional arts include Apsara dance, silk weaving, and stone carving.
17) The Cambodian New Year, known as Chaul Chnam Thmey, is a major festival celebrated in mid-April.
18) The country has a rich history dating back to the Khmer Empire, which was at its height during the 9th to 15th centuries.
19) Cambodian people are known for their warmth and hospitality, making it a friendly destination for travelers.
20) Cambodian handicrafts, including silverware, ceramics, and silk products, are popular souvenirs among visitors.

These quick facts provide a glimpse into the culture, history, and natural beauty of Cambodia, a country with a rich heritage and a welcoming spirit.

Updated Cambodia Travel Guide

How To Use This Guide

This Updated Cambodia Travel Guide is designed to assist you in planning and experiencing a memorable journey through the enchanting country of Cambodia. Here are some tips on how to make the most of this guide:

- **Familiarize Yourself:** Start by reading the introduction and the overview of Cambodia to gain a comprehensive understanding of the country's history, culture, and attractions. This will provide you with a solid foundation before delving into the specific sections.
- **Plan Your Itinerary:** Use the table of contents to navigate the guide and identify the sections that align with your interests and travel preferences. Whether you want to explore ancient temples, relax on pristine beaches, or immerse yourself in local culture, the guide offers a variety of topics to choose from.
- **Seek Inspiration:** Take advantage of the suggested itineraries and sample experiences provided in the appendices. These can serve as a starting point to help you structure your own travel plans and make the most of your time in Cambodia.
- **Gather Practical Information:** Throughout the guide, you'll find practical tips, advice, and recommendations on topics such as transportation, accommodations, visa requirements, and safety. Take note of this information and refer back to it as you plan your trip.

- **Dive into Details:** Once you have identified the regions or attractions you wish to explore, read the corresponding sections for in-depth information. Discover the must-see sights, recommended activities, dining options, and accommodation suggestions that suit your preferences and budget.
- **Immerse Yourself:** Use this guide as a reference to immerse yourself in Cambodian culture. Learn about local customs and etiquette, discover traditional arts and performances, and try out basic Khmer phrases to enhance your interactions with the locals.
- **Stay Informed:** Make use of the additional resources provided in the appendices, including recommended reading materials and glossary of common Khmer terms. These resources can further enrich your understanding of Cambodia and enhance your overall travel experience.

Remember that this guide is meant to be a flexible tool that adapts to your individual interests and needs. Feel free to customize your itinerary, seek additional information from reputable sources, and embrace the spontaneity and surprises that come with travel. Let this guide be your companion as you embark on an incredible journey through the wonders of Cambodia.

PLANNING YOUR TRIP

When it comes to visiting Cambodia, careful planning can make all the difference in ensuring a smooth and enjoyable travel experience. This section of the Updated Cambodia Travel Guide provides essential information and tips to help you plan your trip effectively. From determining the best time to visit and understanding visa requirements to managing your finances and choosing transportation options, this section covers all the key aspects of trip planning.

By carefully considering the information provided in this guide, you can optimize your itinerary, make informed decisions, and anticipate any necessary preparations. Whether you're a first-time traveler to Cambodia or a returning visitor, this section equips you with the knowledge and tools to navigate the logistical aspects of your trip, leaving you with more time to immerse yourself in the country's rich history, stunning landscapes, and vibrant culture.

Remember, planning is an essential part of any successful journey, and this guide is here to assist you in creating unforgettable memories as you explore the wonders of Cambodia.

Updated Cambodia Travel Guide

Best Time to Visit

Choosing the best time to visit Cambodia largely depends on your preferences and the type of experience you seek. Cambodia generally experiences a tropical climate, characterized by two distinct seasons: the dry season and the rainy season. Here's a breakdown of the seasons to help you determine the optimal time for your visit:

1. Dry Season (November to April):

The dry season in Cambodia is the peak tourist season, known for its sunny weather and lower chances of rainfall. The months of November to February offer pleasant temperatures and are ideal for exploring the country's renowned temples, such as Angkor Wat. However, it's worth noting that this period can also be crowded, particularly during the Christmas and New Year holidays. March and April tend to be hotter, with temperatures soaring above 30°C (86°F), but they offer fewer crowds and are a great time to explore coastal regions like Sihanoukville and its surrounding islands.

2. Rainy Season (May to October):

The rainy season in Cambodia brings lush green landscapes and occasional showers, usually in the form of short downpours that don't hinder travel plans significantly. The months of May and June mark the beginning of the rainy season, with intermittent rains and fewer tourists. The countryside is at its most beautiful during this time, with rice paddies vibrant and waterfalls flowing abundantly. July to September are considered the wettest months, but they can also be a great time to visit, as the rain brings cooler temperatures and fewer crowds. The Angkor temples are particularly atmospheric during this period, with fewer tourists and a refreshing ambiance.

It's important to note that even during the rainy season, there are still many enjoyable activities and destinations to explore in Cambodia. The weather can be unpredictable, but it often doesn't hinder travel plans significantly, especially if you come prepared with lightweight rain gear and a flexible mindset.

Ultimately, the best time to visit Cambodia depends on your preferences. If you prefer fewer crowds and don't mind occasional rain, the rainy season can be a great opportunity to experience Cambodia's lush landscapes in a more tranquil setting. On the other hand, if you prioritize dry and sunny weather for outdoor activities, the dry season is your best bet.

Consider the specific activities you plan to engage in and the destinations you wish to visit, and choose a time that aligns with your preferences. Regardless of the season, Cambodia's beauty, culture, and warm hospitality are sure to leave a lasting impression on your journey.

Visa Requirements

Before embarking on your trip to Cambodia, it's important to understand the visa requirements to ensure a smooth entry into the country. Here's an overview of the visa options available for most travelers:

1. Visa on Arrival (VoA):

Citizens of most countries can obtain a visa upon arrival at the major international airports in Phnom Penh and Siem Reap, as well as at land border crossings. The visa on arrival allows for a stay of up to 30 days. To obtain the VoA, you will need to present a valid passport (with at least six months of validity remaining) and a passport-sized photo. The visa fee is payable in US dollars in cash.

2. E-Visa:

For added convenience, you can apply for an e-visa online before your trip. The e-visa allows for a single entry and a maximum stay of 30 days. To apply, visit the official Cambodian e-visa website and follow the application process. The e-visa requires a passport-sized photo and a scanned copy of your passport information page. The visa fee, as well as a processing fee, can be paid online.

3. Visa Extensions:

If you wish to extend your stay beyond the initial 30 days, you can apply for a visa extension at the Department of Immigration in Phnom Penh or Siem Reap. Extensions of up to one month are usually granted, but additional fees apply.

It's important to note that visa requirements and regulations can change, so it's advisable to check the official website of the Cambodian Ministry of Foreign Affairs and International Cooperation or consult with your local Cambodian embassy or consulate for the most up-to-date information.

Additionally, it's recommended to ensure your passport has at least six months of validity remaining from the date of entry into Cambodia. Some nationalities may be required to provide additional documents or fulfill specific requirements, so it's essential to research and understand the specific visa regulations that apply to your country of citizenship.

By familiarizing yourself with the visa requirements and obtaining the necessary visa in advance, you can enter Cambodia without any complications and fully enjoy your visit to this captivating country.

Currency and Exchange Rates

The official currency of Cambodia is the Cambodian Riel (KHR), and it coexists with the widely accepted United States Dollar (USD). Here are some key points to know about currency and exchange rates in Cambodia:

- **USD as a Common Currency:** USD is widely used and accepted in Cambodia, particularly in tourist areas, hotels, restaurants, and larger establishments. Many prices, particularly for tourist-related services, are quoted in USD. It's advisable to carry a mix of small denomination USD bills for convenience.
- **Cambodian Riel Usage:** While USD is widely accepted, Cambodian Riel is the official currency, and you'll need Riel for smaller transactions, local markets, street food, and in more rural or remote areas. The use of Riel is also common for receiving change in small amounts, even when the main transaction is conducted in USD.
- **Exchange Rates:** The exchange rate between USD and KHR fluctuates, and it's important to be aware of the prevailing rates. The rates may vary slightly between different money changers, banks, and exchange services. It's advisable to compare rates and transaction fees before exchanging money.

- **Currency Exchange:** Currency exchange services are widely available in major cities and tourist areas. Banks and licensed money changers typically offer competitive rates. It's recommended to exchange currency at authorized and reputable establishments to ensure fair rates and avoid counterfeit currency.
- **ATM Withdrawals:** ATMs are prevalent in urban areas and accept both USD and KHR. Be aware that some ATMs may charge withdrawal fees, and it's advisable to inform your bank about your travel plans to avoid any issues with international transactions.
- **Credit Cards and Traveler's Checks**: Major credit cards are accepted at upscale establishments, hotels, and some restaurants. However, smaller businesses and local markets may prefer cash. Traveler's checks are not widely accepted and can be challenging to exchange.
- **Currency Conversion Tips:** When receiving change or conducting transactions, it's common for businesses to provide a combination of USD and KHR. Familiarize yourself with the currency denominations and keep track of which currency you're using to avoid confusion.

It's important to note that exchange rates and currency usage can vary in different regions of Cambodia, so it's advisable to be prepared with a mix of USD and some Riel when traveling throughout the country.

Updated Cambodia Travel Guide

By understanding the currency dynamics and having a combination of USD and Riel, you'll be well-equipped to handle transactions and enjoy your time in Cambodia with ease.

Health and Safety Tips

When traveling to Cambodia, it's important to prioritize your health and safety to ensure a smooth and enjoyable trip. Here are some key health and safety tips to keep in mind:

I. **Vaccinations:** Before traveling to Cambodia, consult with a healthcare professional or travel clinic to receive the necessary vaccinations. Common recommendations include vaccines for hepatitis A and B, typhoid, tetanus, diphtheria, and measles. Depending on your travel plans and personal health, additional vaccines or medications such as malaria prophylaxis may be advised.

II. **Food and Water Safety:** To avoid foodborne illnesses, consume only well-cooked and freshly prepared food. Stick to bottled water or ensure that the water you drink is boiled or properly treated. It's also wise to avoid consuming raw or unpeeled fruits and vegetables unless they have been thoroughly washed and/or peeled by yourself.

III. **Hygiene Practices:** Practice good hygiene by washing your hands frequently with soap and water or using hand sanitizers, especially before meals and after using the restroom. Carry hand sanitizers or wet wipes for situations where clean water and soap may not be readily available.

IV. **Mosquito-borne Diseases:** Cambodia is known for mosquito-borne diseases such as dengue fever and

malaria. Protect yourself by wearing long sleeves, using mosquito repellents containing DEET, and sleeping under mosquito nets, particularly in high-risk areas or during peak mosquito activity times.
V. **Sun Protection:** Cambodia has a tropical climate with intense sunlight. Protect your skin from harmful UV rays by wearing sunscreen, hats, and sunglasses, and seek shade during the hottest parts of the day.
VI. **Travel Insurance:** Obtain comprehensive travel insurance that covers medical emergencies, trip cancellations, and personal belongings. Ensure that your insurance policy includes coverage for medical evacuation, as it may be necessary in case of serious illness or injury.
VII. **Personal Safety:** Exercise caution and be aware of your surroundings, particularly in crowded tourist areas or when traveling at night. Keep your personal belongings secure, and avoid displaying excessive signs of wealth. Use reliable transportation services and only use licensed taxis or reputable transportation companies.
VIII. **Cultural Sensitivity:** Respect local customs, traditions, and religious sites. Dress modestly when visiting temples and religious sites, and remove your shoes when required. Avoid photographing individuals without their consent, especially monks and religious ceremonies.

By following these health and safety tips, you can ensure a safe and enjoyable experience during your visit to Cambodia.

Updated Cambodia Travel Guide

Remember to stay informed, take necessary precautions, and be respectful of the local culture to make the most of your time in this fascinating country.

Transportation Options

When exploring Cambodia, various transportation options are available to help you navigate the country's diverse landscapes and reach your desired destinations. Here are some common transportation options to consider:

1) **Tuk-tuks:** Tuk-tuks are a popular mode of transportation in Cambodia, especially in urban areas like Phnom Penh and Siem Reap. These motorized three-wheeled vehicles can accommodate a few passengers and are convenient for short distances or exploring city streets. Negotiate the fare before your journey or ensure the driver uses a meter.
2) **Taxis:** Taxis are available in major cities, and they are a comfortable and reliable mode of transportation. Metered taxis are commonly found in Phnom Penh, while in other areas, negotiation is necessary. Using reputable taxi companies or ride-hailing apps like Grab can ensure a fair and safe journey.
3) **Motorbike Taxis:** Known as "motodops," motorbike taxis are popular for short trips and navigating through traffic quickly. It's important to wear a helmet and agree on the fare beforehand. While convenient, exercise caution as motorbike taxis may not be suitable for longer distances or travelers with heavy luggage.
4) **Rental Cars:** Renting a car can offer flexibility and convenience, particularly for exploring remote areas or planning day trips. International and local car rental

companies operate in major cities. Ensure you have an international driving permit and are familiar with local traffic regulations. Driving in Cambodia can be challenging due to road conditions and traffic congestion, so exercise caution.

5) **Buses:** Cambodia has a network of intercity buses connecting major cities and popular tourist destinations. Several bus companies offer different levels of comfort and pricing options. VIP buses with air conditioning and sleeper buses for overnight journeys are available. It's advisable to book in advance, especially during peak travel seasons.

6) **Ferries and Boats:** Cambodia's river systems and coastal areas provide opportunities for boat travel. Ferries and boats operate along the Mekong River, Tonle Sap Lake, and to popular destinations like Koh Rong and Koh Rong Samloem islands. It's important to check schedules and safety conditions, particularly during the rainy season.

7) **Domestic Flights:** Domestic flights connect major cities in Cambodia, providing a time-efficient option for covering long distances. Airlines such as Cambodia Angkor Air and Bassaka Air operate domestic routes. However, keep in mind that flights may be limited and relatively more expensive compared to other modes of transportation.

Consider your travel itinerary, budget, and personal preferences when choosing transportation options in Cambodia. It's advisable to research reputable service

Updated Cambodia Travel Guide

providers, confirm fares in advance, and stay informed about any safety considerations to ensure a comfortable and hassle-free journey throughout this captivating country.

Updated Cambodia Travel Guide

EXPLORING PHNOM PENH

Phnom Penh, the capital city of Cambodia, is a vibrant and bustling metropolis that offers a captivating blend of rich history, vibrant culture, and modern developments. Nestled along the banks of the Mekong River, Phnom Penh is a city of contrasts, where traditional Khmer architecture stands alongside contemporary skyscrapers.

As the cultural, political, and economic center of the country, Phnom Penh is a must-visit destination for travelers seeking to delve into Cambodia's past and present. The city is home to numerous captivating attractions, including the iconic Royal Palace, the sacred Wat Phnom, and the poignant Tuol Sleng Genocide Museum. Strolling along the bustling riverside promenade, exploring vibrant markets, and sampling delectable Khmer cuisine are just a few of the experiences that await visitors in this dynamic city.

Phnom Penh's history as the former capital of the Khmer Empire and its turbulent recent past under the Khmer Rouge regime adds depth and significance to its cultural heritage. Today, Phnom Penh is experiencing rapid development, with a thriving arts scene, trendy cafes, and a vibrant nightlife.

Whether you're intrigued by history, fascinated by local culture, or simply seeking to immerse yourself in the lively energy of a bustling city, Phnom Penh offers a wealth of experiences that will leave a lasting impression. Prepare to be captivated by the charm, resilience, and vibrant spirit of Phnom Penh as you embark on an exploration of this captivating Cambodian city.

Updated Cambodia Travel Guide

Top Attractions

Phnom Penh, the capital city of Cambodia, is a treasure trove of cultural landmarks, historical sites, and vibrant attractions. Here are some of the top attractions to explore during your visit to Phnom Penh:

1. **Royal Palace and Silver Pagoda:** The magnificent Royal Palace complex is a must-visit, showcasing stunning Khmer architecture and housing the official residence of the King of Cambodia. Within the complex, the Silver Pagoda, also known as the Temple of the Emerald Buddha, captivates visitors with its intricate silver floor tiles and an awe-inspiring collection of Buddha statues.
2. **Tuol Sleng Genocide Museum (S-21):** Gain insight into Cambodia's dark past at the Tuol Sleng Genocide Museum, formerly a high school turned into a prison during the Khmer Rouge regime. This somber museum exhibits photographs, artifacts, and personal accounts, commemorating the victims of the regime.
3. **Choeung Ek Killing Fields:** Located just outside the city, the Choeung Ek Killing Fields is a memorial site that serves as a poignant reminder of the Khmer Rouge atrocities. Explore the grounds, visit the memorial stupa filled with victims' skulls, and learn about Cambodia's painful history.

4. **Wat Phnom:** Situated atop a small hill, Wat Phnom is the city's oldest temple and holds great cultural significance. This peaceful sanctuary features beautiful gardens, intricate carvings, and a sense of tranquility amidst the bustling city.
5. **National Museum of Cambodia:** Immerse yourself in Cambodian art and history at the National Museum. The museum houses a remarkable collection of sculptures, ceramics, and artifacts, offering insight into the country's ancient past.
6. **Russian Market (Phsar Toul Tom Poung):** Explore the bustling Russian Market, a popular shopping destination known for its vibrant atmosphere and a wide variety of goods, including textiles, handicrafts, and local souvenirs.
7. **Riverside Promenade:** Take a leisurely stroll along the lively riverside promenade, lined with restaurants, cafes, and bars. Enjoy the scenic views of the Mekong River, soak in the atmosphere, and indulge in local street food.

These attractions are just a glimpse of what Phnom Penh has to offer. The city's dynamic blend of history, culture, and modernity ensures an enriching and memorable experience for travelers seeking to explore the heart and soul of Cambodia.

Dining and Nightlife

Phnom Penh offers a vibrant dining and nightlife scene that caters to a variety of tastes and preferences. From traditional Khmer cuisine to international flavors, as well as a mix of casual eateries and upscale restaurants, the city has something to satisfy every palate. Here's a glimpse into the dining and nightlife experiences in Phnom Penh:

Dining

Khmer Cuisine: Indulge in authentic Khmer cuisine, characterized by flavorful dishes such as amok (a coconut-based curry), lok lak (marinated beef stir-fry), and fresh seafood. Visit local markets, street food stalls, or Khmer restaurants to savor the traditional flavors of Cambodia.

- **International Fare:** Phnom Penh boasts a diverse range of international cuisines, including French, Italian, Indian, Japanese, and more. From trendy cafes to fine dining establishments, you'll find a plethora of options to suit your cravings.
- **Riverside Dining:** Enjoy a memorable dining experience along the picturesque riverside promenade. Numerous restaurants and bars offer stunning views of

the Mekong River while serving up a variety of cuisines and refreshing beverages.

Nightlife

- **Pub Street:** Phnom Penh has its own version of the famous Pub Street, offering a lively atmosphere with bars, clubs, and live music venues. Explore the vibrant nightlife scene around Bassac Lane or Street 278, known for its cozy bars and cocktail lounges.

- o **Rooftop Bars:** Experience the city's skyline from above at one of Phnom Penh's rooftop bars. Enjoy panoramic views, creative cocktails, and a sophisticated ambiance as you unwind and take in the city lights.
- o **Live Music and Performances:** Immerse yourself in the local music scene by catching live performances at venues like Meta House or Oscar's on the Corner. From traditional Khmer music to international acts, there's always something to enjoy.
- o **Night Markets:** For a unique nighttime experience, explore the vibrant night markets in Phnom Penh. These bustling markets offer a blend of shopping, street food, and entertainment, creating a lively and colorful atmosphere.

Phnom Penh's dining and nightlife scene continues to evolve, with new establishments constantly popping up. Whether you prefer a relaxed evening savoring Khmer delicacies or a night of dancing and socializing, Phnom Penh has a wealth of options to ensure a memorable and enjoyable experience.

Shopping Experiences

Phnom Penh offers a vibrant and diverse shopping scene, where visitors can explore traditional markets, modern malls, and boutique shops. From handicrafts and textiles to fashionable clothing and local souvenirs, here are some shopping experiences to enjoy in Phnom Penh:

1. **Russian Market (Phsar Toul Tom Poung):** Known for its bustling atmosphere and extensive variety of goods, the Russian Market is a popular destination for shopping in Phnom Penh. Here, you can find everything from clothing, jewelry, and accessories to antiques, handicrafts, and souvenirs. Be prepared to bargain for the best prices.
2. **Central Market (Phsar Thmei):** Housed in a striking art deco building, Central Market is a landmark in Phnom Penh. It offers a wide range of products, including clothing, electronics, household items, and fresh produce. Explore the vibrant market and soak in the lively atmosphere as you shop for bargains.
3. **Night Markets:** Phnom Penh's night markets provide a unique shopping experience. Stroll through the illuminated stalls, sample local street food, and browse a variety of goods, including clothing, accessories, artwork, and handmade crafts. Phnom

Penh Night Market and Riverside Night Market are popular choices.

4. **Designer Boutiques and Concept Stores:** For those seeking unique and stylish items, Phnom Penh is home to a growing number of designer boutiques and concept stores. Discover local and international brands, fashion-forward clothing, handmade jewelry, and home decor items that reflect Cambodia's contemporary creative scene.
5. **Art Galleries and Artisan Workshops:** Phnom Penh has a thriving arts and crafts scene, with art galleries and artisan workshops showcasing the talent of local artists. Visit these spaces to browse and purchase paintings, sculptures, ceramics, textiles, and other artistic creations.
6. **Modern Malls:** Phnom Penh is home to several modern shopping malls offering a mix of international and local brands, along with entertainment and dining options. Aeon Mall and TK Avenue are popular choices for a modern shopping experience.

When shopping in Phnom Penh, it's always advisable to practice your bargaining skills, compare prices, and be mindful of quality. Whether you're searching for unique souvenirs, fashionable clothing, or exquisite handicrafts, Phnom Penh offers a range of shopping experiences that cater to every taste and budget.

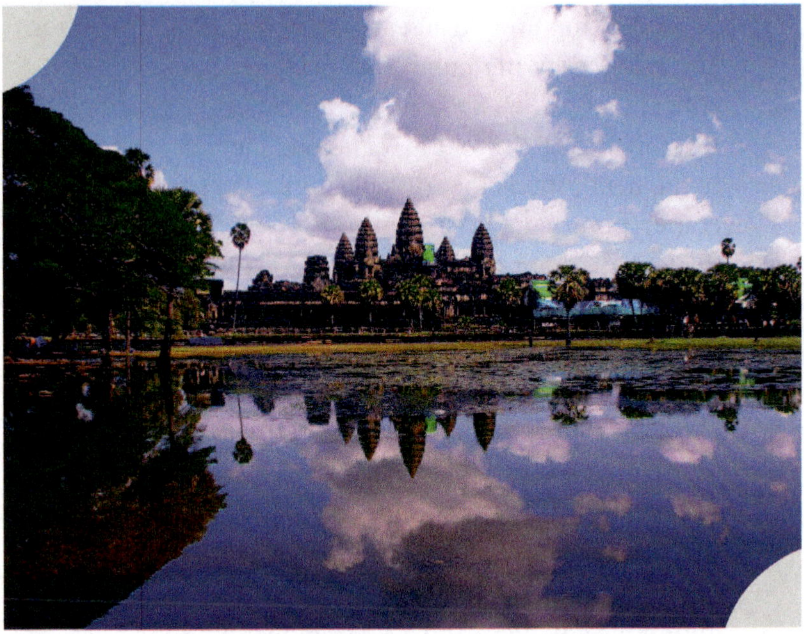

Accommodation Options

Phnom Penh, the capital city of Cambodia, offers a wide range of accommodation options to suit every budget and preference. Whether you're looking for luxury hotels, boutique guesthouses, or budget-friendly hostels, there are plenty of choices available. Here are some popular accommodation options in Phnom Penh:

1. **Luxury Hotels:** Phnom Penh boasts a selection of luxurious hotels that offer world-class amenities, impeccable service, and elegant surroundings. These hotels often feature spacious rooms, swimming pools, spa facilities, fine dining restaurants, and stunning views of the city or riverfront.
2. **Boutique Hotels:** For a more intimate and unique experience, consider staying in one of Phnom Penh's boutique hotels. These properties often have stylish decor, personalized service, and a distinct character. Boutique hotels in Phnom Penh can range from charming colonial-style villas to contemporary designs that blend traditional and modern elements.
3. **Mid-range Hotels:** There is a wide range of mid-range hotels available in Phnom Penh, offering comfortable accommodations at affordable prices. These hotels typically provide modern amenities, well-appointed rooms, and convenient locations within the city.

4. **Guesthouses and Homestays:** Phnom Penh is dotted with guesthouses and homestays, offering a more local and immersive experience. These budget-friendly options provide basic accommodations with private or shared facilities. Staying in a guesthouse or homestay can be an excellent way to connect with the local culture and receive personalized recommendations from your hosts.
5. **Hostels:** Phnom Penh has a thriving backpacker scene, and hostels are a popular choice for budget travelers. These budget accommodations offer dormitory-style rooms and communal facilities, creating a social and vibrant atmosphere. Hostels in Phnom Penh often organize group activities, city tours, and provide a platform for meeting fellow travelers.

When selecting accommodation in Phnom Penh, consider factors such as location, amenities, and the overall ambiance that aligns with your travel preferences. It's advisable to book in advance, especially during peak tourist seasons, to secure your desired accommodation.

Updated Cambodia Travel Guide

SIEM REAP AND ANGKOR WAT

Siem Reap, a charming city in northwestern Cambodia, is a gateway to the majestic temples of Angkor, including the iconic Angkor Wat. This historical and cultural treasure draws visitors from around the world, offering a glimpse into the grandeur and architectural brilliance of the Khmer Empire.

Angkor Wat, the largest religious monument in the world, is the crown jewel of Siem Reap's attractions. Its intricate carvings, towering spires, and vast complex of temples are a testament to the Khmer civilization's artistic and engineering prowess. As the sun rises or sets over Angkor Wat, the temple's silhouette against the colorful sky creates a breathtaking spectacle that leaves visitors in awe.

Beyond Angkor Wat, Siem Reap has much to offer. The city itself is vibrant, with a mix of traditional Khmer architecture, bustling markets, lively street food scenes, and a growing array of contemporary cafes, restaurants, and bars. Exploring the Old Market (Phsar Chas), wandering along Pub Street, and sampling the flavors of Khmer cuisine are among the many experiences to savor in Siem Reap.

Moreover, Siem Reap serves as a base for further exploration of the Angkor Archaeological Park, which encompasses numerous temples and ruins, each with its own unique charm and historical significance. From the enigmatic faces of Bayon Temple to the intricate carvings of Banteay Srei, visitors can delve deep into Cambodia's ancient history and marvel at the cultural heritage preserved within these ancient structures.

Siem Reap and Angkor Wat are a testament to Cambodia's rich history, architectural splendor, and spiritual significance. A visit to this captivating destination promises an unforgettable journey into the heart of the Khmer Empire's legacy.

Updated Cambodia Travel Guide

Exploring the Angkor Archaeological Park

The Angkor Archaeological Park in Cambodia is a UNESCO World Heritage site and a must-visit destination for history enthusiasts, cultural explorers, and adventure seekers. Spanning over 400 square kilometers, this vast complex is home to hundreds of temples and ruins that showcase the grandeur and artistic brilliance of the Khmer Empire. Here's a comprehensive guide to help you make the most of your visit to the Angkor Archaeological Park.

1. **Angkor Wat:** Start your exploration with the iconic Angkor Wat, the largest religious monument in the world. Dedicated to the Hindu god Vishnu and later transformed into a Buddhist temple, Angkor Wat is renowned for its intricate carvings, towering spires, and stunning bas-reliefs. Explore the temple's multiple levels, admire the stunning sunrise or sunset views, and immerse yourself in the rich historical and spiritual atmosphere.
2. **Bayon Temple:** Known for its enigmatic smiling faces, Bayon Temple is one of the most mesmerizing and distinctive structures in the Angkor complex. Explore the labyrinthine corridors and climb the steep staircases to encounter the serene faces carved into the

stone towers. The intricate bas-reliefs depict scenes of everyday life, battles, and mythical stories.
3. **Ta Prohm:** Venture into the enchanting world of Ta Prohm, where nature and ancient architecture intertwine. This temple is famous for its atmospheric and photogenic setting, with giant trees growing among the ruins, creating a captivating blend of ancient stones and sprawling roots. Ta Prohm's appearance in the movie "Lara Croft: Tomb Raider" has added to its allure.
4. **Banteay Srei:** Considered the jewel of Khmer art, Banteay Srei is a temple known for its exquisite pink sandstone carvings. The intricate details and delicate craftsmanship are truly awe-inspiring. Despite its relatively smaller size, Banteay Srei is a gem that should not be missed.
5. **Preah Khan:** Explore the sprawling complex of Preah Khan, which was once a major religious and administrative center. Wander through the ancient hallways, marvel at the towering trees that engulf the structures, and discover hidden corners and intricately carved doorways. The atmosphere here is both mysterious and serene.
6. **Terrace of the Elephants**: Marvel at the grandeur of the Terrace of the Elephants, which served as a viewing platform for royal processions and ceremonies. Admire the intricate carvings of elephants, garudas, and other mythical creatures that adorn the terrace walls. This expansive structure offers insights into the grandeur of the Khmer Empire.

7. **Angkor Thom:** Visit the ancient city of Angkor Thom, which served as the capital of the Khmer Empire. Enter through the grand South Gate and explore the various temples and structures within the city, including the aforementioned Bayon Temple, Terrace of the Elephants, and the Terrace of the Leper King. Renting a bike or hiring a tuk-tuk driver is a convenient way to navigate the vast grounds of Angkor Thom.
8. **Lesser-known Temples:** While the main temples mentioned above are popular highlights, the Angkor Archaeological Park is also home to several lesser-known temples waiting to be discovered. These include Ta Som, Pre Rup, Beng Mealea, and many more. Exploring these off-the-beaten-path temples allows for a more intimate and peaceful experience, with fewer crowds and a chance to immerse yourself in the raw beauty of these ancient structures.

Tips for Exploring the Angkor Archaeological Park, Cambodia

- ✓ **Plan your visit:** Research the temples you want to see and plan your itinerary in advance. Consider the distance between temples and their opening hours.
- ✓ **Start early:** Beat the crowds and experience the temples in a quieter atmosphere by starting your visit early in the morning.
- ✓ **Dress appropriately:** Remember to dress respectfully, covering your shoulders and knees. Wear comfortable clothing suitable for the tropical climate.
- ✓ **Stay hydrated:** Carry a water bottle and stay hydrated throughout your visit. The Cambodian weather can be hot and humid.
- ✓ **Engage a guide:** Consider hiring a knowledgeable guide who can provide historical and cultural insights to enhance your experience.
- ✓ **Respect the sites:** Follow the rules and regulations of the park, avoid climbing restricted areas, and be mindful of preserving the temples.
- ✓ **Take breaks:** The park is extensive, so take breaks and rest when needed. Pace yourself to avoid fatigue.
- ✓ **Capture memories responsibly:** Take photographs responsibly, being mindful of other visitors and respecting any restrictions on photography.

Updated Cambodia Travel Guide

By following these tips, you can make the most of your visit to the Angkor Archaeological Park and create lasting memories of this remarkable historical site.

Other Attractions in Siem Reap

While the Angkor Archaeological Park steals the spotlight in Siem Reap, the city offers a range of other attractions that are worth exploring. From cultural experiences to natural wonders, here are some additional attractions to consider during your visit:

1. **Floating Villages:** Take a boat tour to the floating villages on the Tonle Sap Lake, southeast of Siem Reap. Experience the unique lifestyle of the local communities who live in stilted houses and rely on fishing as their primary livelihood. Witness the daily activities of the villagers and gain insight into their resilient way of life.
2. **Artisans Angkor:** Visit Artisans Angkor, a social enterprise that promotes traditional Khmer craftsmanship. Explore their workshops and witness skilled artisans creating intricate stone carvings, woodwork, silk weaving, and other handicrafts. The center also features a showroom where you can purchase high-quality, locally-made products.
3. **Phare, The Cambodian Circus:** Witness the mesmerizing performances at Phare, The Cambodian Circus. This contemporary circus showcases the talents

of young Cambodian artists who deliver an entertaining blend of acrobatics, dance, theater, and storytelling. The shows are not only visually impressive but also support a social cause by providing training and employment opportunities to underprivileged youth.

4. **Cambodian Cultural Village:** Immerse yourself in Cambodian culture at the Cambodian Cultural Village, which offers a glimpse into the country's diverse traditions and heritage. Explore the traditional houses, watch cultural performances, and learn about Cambodian customs, dances, and rituals. It's a great opportunity to deepen your understanding of the country's rich cultural tapestry.

5. **Phnom Kulen National Park:** Escape the city and venture to Phnom Kulen National Park, located approximately 50 kilometers from Siem Reap. This picturesque area is known for its natural beauty, waterfalls, and historical sites. Hike to the top of the mountain to visit the sacred Phnom Kulen pagoda and discover ancient temples, including the famous River of a Thousand Lingas.

6. **Siem Reap Night Market:** Experience the vibrant atmosphere of the Siem Reap Night Market. Stroll through the bustling stalls, shop for souvenirs, handicrafts, and clothing, and indulge in local street food. The market comes alive in the evening, offering a lively and colorful ambiance.

These attractions offer a diverse range of experiences beyond the temples of Angkor. From immersing yourself in local culture to enjoying natural wonders and vibrant markets, Siem Reap has something to captivate every traveler.

Local Cuisine and Dining Recommendations

Siem Reap, the gateway to the magnificent Angkor Wat, offers a diverse culinary scene that showcases the rich flavors and unique ingredients of Cambodian cuisine. From street food stalls to upscale restaurants, here are some dining recommendations to indulge in the local culinary delights:

1) **Amok:** Don't miss the chance to try Amok, one of Cambodia's signature dishes. This flavorful curry is typically made with fish, chicken, or tofu, cooked in a fragrant blend of spices, coconut milk, and kroeung (a traditional Khmer spice paste). Served with steamed rice, Amok is a must-try dish for its harmonious combination of spices and creamy texture.
2) **Fish Amok:** Located in the heart of Siem Reap, Fish Amok is a popular restaurant that specializes in its namesake dish. Their Fish Amok is prepared using the freshest ingredients and served in a coconut shell, presenting a visually appealing and delicious dining experience.
3) **Khmer BBQ:** Experience the interactive dining concept of Khmer BBQ at one of the local night markets. Choose from an array of marinated meats, seafood, and vegetables, and grill them at your table. This enjoyable dining experience allows you to savor

the smoky flavors and customize your meal according to your preferences.

4) **Street Food Stalls:** Siem Reap's bustling street food scene is a paradise for food lovers. Explore the local markets such as Psar Chas (Old Market) and Psar Leu (Big Market), where you can find an assortment of authentic Cambodian dishes such as noodle soups, grilled meats, and delicious desserts like sticky rice with mango.

5) **Cuisine Wat Damnak:** For a more upscale dining experience, consider Cuisine Wat Damnak, a renowned restaurant that showcases refined Cambodian cuisine. The menu features seasonal ingredients sourced locally, ensuring fresh and flavorful dishes that pay homage to Cambodian culinary traditions with a modern twist.

6) **Pub Street:** Siem Reap's vibrant Pub Street is not only known for its nightlife but also for its diverse dining options. From traditional Khmer restaurants to international cuisines, there's something to suit every palate. Explore the lively street and discover hidden gems offering delectable dishes.

Remember to venture beyond the popular tourist areas and explore the local neighborhoods, where you can discover smaller, family-run restaurants serving authentic Cambodian dishes. Embrace the flavors, spices, and unique culinary traditions of Cambodia to truly immerse yourself in the local dining scene while visiting Siem Reap and the awe-inspiring Angkor Wat.

Updated Cambodia Travel Guide

Accommodation Options

Siem Reap, being the gateway to the majestic temples of Angkor Wat, offers a wide range of accommodation options to suit every traveler's needs and preferences. From luxury resorts to budget-friendly guesthouses, here are some recommendations for finding the perfect place to stay:

1) **Luxury Resorts:** Siem Reap is home to several luxury resorts that provide a lavish and indulgent experience. These resorts often feature spacious rooms, elegant amenities, beautiful gardens, and relaxing spa facilities. Many of them offer stunning views of the surrounding landscapes, providing a tranquil setting for your stay.
2) **Boutique Hotels:** Siem Reap boasts a variety of charming boutique hotels, each with its own unique style and character. These smaller accommodations offer personalized service, cozy rooms, and a more intimate ambiance. They often showcase traditional Khmer architecture and design, providing an authentic and immersive experience.
3) **Mid-Range Hotels:** There are numerous mid-range hotels in Siem Reap that strike a balance between affordability and comfort. These hotels offer comfortable rooms, essential amenities, and friendly service. They are a great option for travelers seeking a comfortable stay without breaking the bank.

4) **Guesthouses and Hostels:** For budget-conscious travelers, guesthouses and hostels provide affordable accommodation options in Siem Reap. These establishments typically offer dormitory-style rooms or private rooms with shared facilities. They are a popular choice for backpackers and solo travelers looking for a social atmosphere and cost-effective lodging.
5) **Eco-Lodges:** For those seeking a more sustainable and eco-friendly accommodation experience, Siem Reap has a selection of eco-lodges. These lodges prioritize environmentally conscious practices, such as using renewable energy, supporting local communities, and promoting responsible tourism. Staying at an eco-lodge allows you to minimize your environmental footprint while enjoying a unique and nature-centric experience.

When choosing accommodation in Siem Reap, consider factors such as proximity to the Angkor temples, accessibility to the city center, and the facilities and services that are important to you. It's advisable to book in advance, especially during peak tourist seasons, to secure your preferred choice of accommodation.

COASTAL AND ISLAND GETAWAYS

While Siem Reap and Angkor Wat may steal the spotlight in Cambodia, the country is also home to beautiful coastal areas and stunning islands that offer a tranquil and idyllic escape. Cambodia's coastal region is known for its pristine beaches, crystal-clear waters, and laid-back atmosphere. From relaxing on the sandy shores to exploring marine life through snorkeling and diving, these coastal and island getaways provide a different side of Cambodia's natural beauty.

Sihanoukville, located on the Gulf of Thailand, is a popular coastal destination that offers a range of beachfront resorts, seafood restaurants, and vibrant nightlife. The nearby islands of Koh Rong and Koh Rong Samloem are known for their white sandy beaches, turquoise waters, and lush tropical landscapes.

For a quieter and more secluded experience, Koh Tonsay (Rabbit Island) and Koh Thmei are perfect choices. These islands offer a serene and untouched environment where you can unwind, enjoy nature, and disconnect from the hustle and bustle of everyday life.

Whether you're seeking relaxation, water activities, or simply the beauty of untouched landscapes, Cambodia's coastal and island getaways provide an opportunity to escape to a tropical paradise.

Sihanoukville

Sihanoukville, located on the southwestern coast of Cambodia, is a popular beach destination that attracts both locals and international travelers. This vibrant coastal city offers a combination of pristine beaches, lively nightlife, and a relaxed atmosphere, making it an ideal getaway for beach lovers and sun seekers.

The main attraction of Sihanoukville is its beautiful beaches. From the bustling Serendipity Beach with its array of restaurants, bars, and water activities, to the tranquil Otres Beach known for its laid-back vibe and golden sands, there is a beach for every preference. Relax on the sun-drenched shores, take a dip in the clear turquoise waters, or indulge in water sports like snorkeling, scuba diving, and kayaking.

Sihanoukville also serves as a gateway to the nearby islands, including Koh Rong and Koh Rong Samloem. These islands offer a more secluded and pristine beach experience, with pristine white sands and crystal-clear waters. Take a boat trip to these islands to explore their untouched beauty, go hiking through lush jungles, or simply unwind in a hammock with a refreshing coconut drink.

In addition to its natural beauty, Sihanoukville boasts a vibrant nightlife scene. The city comes alive after sunset, with a variety of beach bars, clubs, and restaurants offering live music, dancing, and delicious seafood feasts. Experience the lively atmosphere and mingle with fellow travelers while enjoying a cocktail or sampling local delicacies.

Whether you seek relaxation on the beach, adventurous water activities, or a vibrant nightlife, Sihanoukville has something for everyone. It's a destination that offers a blend of natural beauty, cultural experiences, and a tropical ambiance that will leave you rejuvenated and captivated by Cambodia's coastal charm.

Koh Rong and Koh Rong Samloem

Koh Rong and Koh Rong Samloem are two stunning islands off the coast of Sihanoukville, Cambodia, known for their pristine beaches, turquoise waters, and untouched natural beauty. These islands offer a serene and idyllic escape from the hustle and bustle of everyday life, attracting travelers seeking relaxation, tranquility, and a true tropical paradise experience.

Koh Rong is the larger and more developed of the two islands, offering a range of accommodation options, restaurants, and activities. Long Beach, located on the southwestern coast, is a popular spot with its powdery white sand and clear waters, perfect for swimming and sunbathing. Explore the island's lush jungles, go snorkeling or diving to discover the vibrant marine life, or simply enjoy the breathtaking sunset views from one of the beachfront bars.

Koh Rong Samloem, on the other hand, is known for its quieter and more pristine atmosphere. This island is an ideal choice for those seeking a secluded and untouched beach experience. Saracen Bay is the main beach on Koh Rong Samloem, offering a tranquil setting and stunning vistas. Unwind in a hammock, stroll along the shore, or take a boat trip to discover hidden coves and snorkeling spots around the island.

Both islands boast crystal-clear waters, making them perfect for snorkeling and diving. Explore the vibrant coral reefs teeming with colorful marine life, including tropical fish, sea turtles, and even bioluminescent plankton that create a magical glow in the water at night.

With their natural beauty, pristine beaches, and laid-back ambiance, Koh Rong and Koh Rong Samloem are ideal destinations for those seeking an authentic tropical island experience in Cambodia. Whether you want to relax, explore underwater wonders, or simply embrace the serenity of a secluded beach, these islands offer a truly unforgettable escape.

Updated Cambodia Travel Guide

Kep and Kampot

Kep and Kampot are two charming towns located in the southern region of Cambodia, known for their relaxed atmosphere, scenic landscapes, and delicious culinary offerings. These destinations offer a different side of Cambodia, where you can experience the tranquility of coastal life and immerse yourself in the country's rich history and culture.

Kep, often referred to as the "Riviera of Cambodia," is renowned for its seafood and stunning coastline. The town is famous for its crab market, where you can savor freshly caught crabs prepared in various mouthwatering dishes. Take a stroll along the waterfront promenade, explore the nearby Rabbit Island (Koh Tonsay), or relax on the sandy beaches while enjoying breathtaking views of the Gulf of Thailand.

A short distance from Kep, you'll find the charming town of Kampot, nestled along the banks of the Kampong Bay River. Kampot is known for its French colonial architecture, pepper plantations, and scenic riverfront setting. Explore the town's streets lined with colorful colonial buildings, visit local pepper farms to learn about the region's renowned Kampot pepper, or take a boat trip along the river to witness the picturesque landscapes and limestone karsts.

Both Kep and Kampot offer a range of outdoor activities, including kayaking, cycling, and hiking. Discover the nearby Bokor National Park, where you can explore lush forests, visit waterfalls, and enjoy panoramic views from the Bokor Hill Station.

In addition to their natural beauty, Kep and Kampot boast a laid-back vibe and a thriving food scene. Indulge in the local delicacies, from fresh seafood and delectable pepper-infused dishes to the famous Kampot durian, known for its unique flavor.

Whether you're seeking relaxation, culinary delights, or a blend of history and natural beauty, Kep and Kampot offer a delightful escape from the bustling cities and provide a glimpse into the serene coastal life of Cambodia.

Updated Cambodia Travel Guide

Beach Activities and Water Sports

The coastal and island getaways of Cambodia offer not only pristine beaches and stunning landscapes but also a wide array of beach activities and water sports to make your visit truly memorable. Whether you're seeking relaxation or adventure, these destinations provide an ideal playground for aquatic enthusiasts.

One of the popular beach activities in Cambodia is swimming in the crystal-clear waters. Dive into the turquoise depths, cool off from the tropical heat, and embrace the refreshing sensation of the ocean. The calm and gentle waters of the coastal areas are suitable for swimmers of all levels, making it a perfect spot for families and leisurely swims.

Snorkeling is another favorite activity, allowing you to explore the vibrant underwater world teeming with colorful coral reefs and diverse marine life. Put on your mask and fins, and venture into the clear waters to discover an abundance of tropical fish, seahorses, and other fascinating sea creatures. Some of the best snorkeling spots can be found near the islands of Koh Rong, Koh Rong Samloem, and Koh Tonsay.

For those seeking more exhilarating experiences, diving opportunities abound in Cambodia's coastal areas. Discover the hidden treasures beneath the surface, as dive sites offer an opportunity to explore coral gardens, underwater caves, and even shipwrecks. Whether you're a beginner or an experienced diver, there are dive centers in places like Sihanoukville and Koh Rong that offer professional instruction and guided dives.

Watersports enthusiasts will also find plenty of options to satisfy their adventurous spirit. Jet skiing, kayaking, paddleboarding, and banana boat rides are available at many beachfront resorts and rental shops. Feel the thrill of speeding across the waves on a jet ski or challenge yourself to balance on a paddleboard as you navigate the calm coastal waters.

Fishing enthusiasts can embark on fishing trips, either joining local fishermen to experience traditional fishing techniques or trying their luck with sport fishing for larger game fish such as barracuda or sailfish.

Whether you prefer leisurely beach activities or adrenaline-pumping water sports, the coastal and island getaways of Cambodia offer a multitude of options to suit every taste. Immerse yourself in the natural beauty of the coastline, embrace the warm waters, and create unforgettable memories as you explore the rich marine environments and engage in exciting aquatic adventures.

EXPLORING THE COUNTRYSIDE

Beyond its renowned temples, beaches, and cities, Cambodia's countryside is a treasure trove waiting to be discovered. The rural landscapes of this Southeast Asian nation are dotted with picturesque villages, lush rice fields, and a rich cultural heritage. Exploring the countryside of Cambodia offers a unique opportunity to experience the authentic local way of life, immerse yourself in nature, and discover hidden gems off the beaten path.

Venture outside the urban centers and embrace the tranquility of the countryside. Take a leisurely bike ride through the rural villages, where you can witness locals going about their daily activities, encounter friendly smiles, and gain insights into traditional crafts, such as silk weaving or pottery making.

Explore the verdant rice fields, where you can witness the traditional farming practices that have been passed down through generations. Marvel at the vibrant green paddies and learn about the importance of rice cultivation in Cambodian culture and economy.

Visit traditional markets, known as "phsar," where locals gather to sell fresh produce, handicrafts, and local delicacies. Experience the vibrant atmosphere, savor the flavors of Cambodian street food, and engage in friendly interactions with the locals.

Immerse yourself in the natural beauty of Cambodia's countryside by visiting national parks and nature reserves. Discover waterfalls, trek through lush forests, and spot exotic wildlife, such as gibbons, elephants, and a variety of bird species.

Exploring the countryside of Cambodia provides a deeper understanding of the country's heritage, culture, and natural wonders. It allows you to connect with the warmth and hospitality of the Cambodian people while embracing the serenity of rural landscapes. So, step off the well-trodden path and embark on a journey to explore the hidden charms of Cambodia's countryside.

Battambang

Nestled in the northwest region of Cambodia, Battambang is a charming city known for its rich history, French colonial architecture, and artistic scene. This off-the-beaten-path destination offers a glimpse into authentic Cambodian life and provides visitors with a unique cultural experience.

Battambang's colonial-era buildings, wide boulevards, and charming riverside promenade showcase its French influence and make for pleasant strolls through the city. Take a leisurely bike ride or a tuk-tuk tour to explore the city's architectural gems, including the Provincial Hall, Central Market, and the Governor's Residence.

One of the highlights of Battambang is its thriving art scene. The city is home to numerous art galleries, studios, and a vibrant performing arts community. Explore the local art scene by visiting galleries showcasing contemporary and traditional Cambodian art or catch a traditional dance performance at the Phare Ponleu Selpak Circus School.

Battambang is also famous for its ancient temples and pagodas. Wat Banan, also known as the "miniature Angkor Wat," is a must-visit site with its hilltop location and panoramic views of the surrounding countryside. Wat Ek Phnom, another significant temple, features a well-preserved 11th-century sandstone structure and a peaceful atmosphere.

For a unique experience, hop on the Bamboo Train (Norry), a simple and traditional form of transportation. This makeshift railway system takes you through scenic countryside views and provides an exhilarating ride.

Food lovers will delight in the culinary offerings of Battambang. The city is known for its delicious street food, offering a variety of local delicacies such as fried noodles, grilled skewers, and flavorful soups. Don't miss the opportunity to try the famous Battambang bamboo sticky rice, a local specialty that is both tasty and visually appealing.

Battambang's surrounding countryside is also worth exploring. Take a boat ride along the tranquil Sangkae River, visit nearby villages known for their traditional crafts, or witness the production of Cambodia's famous rice wine.

With its blend of history, art, and local culture, Battambang offers a unique and authentic Cambodian experience. Whether you're wandering through the streets admiring the architecture, exploring ancient temples, immersing yourself in the local art scene, or savoring the flavors of Cambodian cuisine, Battambang is a destination that will captivate and leave you with lasting memories.

Kampong Cham

Located along the banks of the Mekong River in eastern Cambodia, Kampong Cham is a charming town known for its rich history, scenic landscapes, and authentic local experiences. As the third-largest city in Cambodia, Kampong Cham offers a blend of urban conveniences and a laid-back rural atmosphere, making it an ideal destination for travelers seeking a glimpse into traditional Cambodian life.

One of the main attractions in Kampong Cham is the iconic Bamboo Bridge. This impressive structure, made entirely of bamboo and stretching over the Mekong River, is rebuilt every year after the rainy season. Walking across the bridge provides a unique perspective of the river and offers picturesque views of the surrounding countryside.

For history enthusiasts, Kampong Cham is home to several important historical sites. Wat Nokor Bachey, a 12th-century temple, is a prominent landmark known for its intricate carvings and peaceful ambiance. Explore the temple complex and discover the fusion of Hindu and Buddhist influences in its architecture.

The nearby countryside of Kampong Cham offers opportunities to experience traditional rural life. Take a bicycle or motorcycle ride through scenic landscapes of rice paddies, palm tree groves, and quaint villages. Engage with friendly locals, witness their daily activities, and learn about traditional crafts, such as silk weaving and pottery making.

Kampong Cham is also known for its lively markets, where you can immerse yourself in the vibrant local culture. Visit the central market to browse a variety of goods, from fresh produce to traditional handicrafts. Don't forget to sample some local street food and taste the flavors of Cambodia.

For a tranquil escape, head to the tranquil island of Koh Pen, accessible by a short ferry ride. Explore the island's picturesque countryside, visit temples, and relax along the riverside.

Whether you're interested in history, cultural immersion, or simply seeking a peaceful retreat, Kampong Cham offers a delightful blend of experiences. From its historical sites to its rural charm, this riverside town invites you to discover the authentic side of Cambodia and create lasting memories.

Updated Cambodia Travel Guide

Kratie and the Irrawaddy Dolphins

Nestled on the banks of the Mekong River in northeastern Cambodia, Kratie is a small town renowned for its peaceful atmosphere and its unique inhabitants—the Irrawaddy dolphins. This picturesque destination offers visitors a chance to witness the fascinating marine life and explore the tranquil countryside.

The highlight of Kratie is undoubtedly the Irrawaddy dolphins, a critically endangered species that inhabits the Mekong River. Take a boat trip along the river to encounter these gentle creatures in their natural habitat. Watch as they swim, surface, and play in the water, creating magical moments that will leave you in awe. The sightings of these rare dolphins are not only captivating but also contribute to the conservation efforts aimed at protecting these magnificent creatures.

Apart from dolphin watching, Kratie offers opportunities to immerse yourself in the rural Cambodian way of life. Explore the surrounding countryside, where you can cycle through picturesque landscapes, visit local villages, and witness traditional farming practices. Interact with friendly locals, learn about their daily activities, and gain insights into their culture and customs.

One of the must-visit sites in Kratie is the 100-Column Pagoda, also known as Wat Rokakandal. This unique temple is named after its design, featuring 100 columns adorned with colorful decorations and intricate carvings. Take a moment to appreciate the architectural beauty and enjoy the serene atmosphere.

To experience the local culinary delights, don't miss the chance to visit the vibrant Kratie Market. This bustling marketplace offers a wide range of fresh produce, street food, and local snacks. Indulge in the flavors of Cambodian cuisine and savor the unique dishes that reflect the region's culinary traditions.

For nature enthusiasts, a visit to the nearby Koh Trong Island is highly recommended. Take a boat ride to this peaceful island, where you can explore charming villages, ride bicycles through fruit orchards, and witness the scenic beauty of the Mekong River.

Kratie and its enchanting Irrawaddy dolphins provide a tranquil escape from the hustle and bustle of city life. Whether you're seeking a close encounter with rare marine life, a glimpse into local culture, or a peaceful retreat in nature, Kratie offers a serene and unforgettable experience in the heart of Cambodia.

Mondulkiri and Ratanakiri

Tucked away in the northeastern highlands of Cambodia, Mondulkiri and Ratanakiri are two captivating provinces that offer an authentic and off-the-beaten-path experience for travelers. These remote regions are known for their pristine natural beauty, rich ethnic diversity, and opportunities for outdoor adventures.

Mondulkiri is a haven for nature enthusiasts. Its lush landscapes are adorned with rolling hills, cascading waterfalls, and dense forests. Explore the Mondulkiri Protected Forest, home to diverse wildlife such as elephants, gibbons, and various bird species. Trek through the forested trails, visit picturesque waterfalls like the Sen Monorom Waterfall, and take in the breathtaking scenery.

Ratanakiri, on the other hand, is renowned for its stunning volcanic lakes, tribal communities, and gemstone mines. Visit the mesmerizing Yeak Laom Lake, nestled within a volcanic crater, where you can swim in the clear waters or simply relax in the tranquil surroundings. Immerse yourself in the vibrant culture of the indigenous hill tribes like the Jarai and Kreung, who have preserved their traditions and unique way of life for generations.

Both Mondulkiri and Ratanakiri offer opportunities for eco-tourism and outdoor activities. Embark on a trekking adventure to explore remote villages, interact with the local communities, and learn about their customs and traditions. Discover the traditional art of elephant trekking, where you can ride these majestic creatures through the forested trails. Experience the thrill of zip-lining across the treetops or embark on a wildlife spotting expedition in search of rare and exotic species.

For those seeking relaxation, both provinces boast serene retreats and eco-lodges nestled amidst nature. Unwind in tranquil surroundings, surrounded by the sounds of the forest and the melodies of birds. Engage in wellness activities such as yoga or meditation, or simply enjoy a rejuvenating massage in the midst of nature's embrace.

Mondulkiri and Ratanakiri offer a unique glimpse into Cambodia's untamed beauty and cultural diversity. With their unspoiled landscapes, welcoming communities, and abundant natural wonders, these provinces provide a truly immersive and unforgettable experience for those seeking an off-the-beaten-path adventure.

Updated Cambodia Travel Guide

Eco-Tourism and Nature Reserves

Cambodia is blessed with a diverse range of ecosystems and an abundance of natural wonders, making it a perfect destination for eco-tourism enthusiasts and nature lovers. The country is committed to preserving its pristine landscapes, promoting sustainable practices, and providing opportunities for visitors to appreciate its unique flora, fauna, and biodiversity.

One of the prominent eco-tourism destinations in Cambodia is the Cardamom Mountains, a vast and biodiverse region spanning across several provinces. This protected area is home to dense rainforests, rare wildlife, and stunning waterfalls. Explore the trails on foot or by bike, and embark on guided treks to encounter elusive species like the Asian elephant, clouded leopard, and numerous bird species.

Another gem for nature enthusiasts is the Preah Monivong Bokor National Park. Located in the southern part of the country, this park offers a range of activities, including hiking, wildlife spotting, and exploring the remnants of French colonial buildings. From the mist-shrouded mountains to the lush vegetation, this park provides a serene retreat in the midst of nature's beauty.

For those interested in birdwatching, the Tmatboey Community-Owned Reserve is a must-visit destination. This community-driven initiative is dedicated to conserving the habitat of the critically endangered Giant Ibis and other bird species. Guided tours and homestay experiences provide visitors with a unique opportunity to learn about conservation efforts and support local communities.

In the heart of Cambodia lies the Tonle Sap Biosphere Reserve, a vast freshwater lake and wetland area that supports a rich ecosystem and sustains numerous communities. Take a boat tour to explore the floating villages, observe the diverse birdlife, and gain insights into the local way of life.

Cambodia's commitment to eco-tourism is further exemplified by the establishment of the Koh Kong Conservation Corridor. This conservation initiative aims to protect the country's coastal and marine resources, including coral reefs, mangroves, and seagrass beds. Visitors can engage in various activities such as snorkeling, kayaking, and learning about marine conservation efforts.

By promoting eco-tourism and protecting its natural reserves, Cambodia provides a unique opportunity for travelers to connect with nature, support local communities, and contribute to conservation efforts. Whether it's exploring the rainforests, observing rare wildlife, or experiencing sustainable community initiatives, Cambodia's eco-tourism offerings are sure to leave a lasting impression on nature enthusiasts.

PRACTICAL INFORMATION

When planning a trip to Cambodia, it's essential to gather practical information to ensure a smooth and enjoyable experience. This section provides key details about visa requirements, currency, health and safety tips, transportation options, and more. From understanding the best time to visit and obtaining the necessary travel documents to navigating local transportation and staying informed about health precautions, this practical information will help you make informed decisions and be well-prepared for your journey in Cambodia.

Essential Travel Resources

When traveling to Cambodia, it's important to have access to essential travel resources that can enhance your experience and ensure a hassle-free trip. Here are some key resources to consider:

1) **Guidebooks and Online Travel Guides:** Guidebooks such as the one you're reading and online travel guides offer comprehensive information on Cambodia's attractions, accommodations, transportation options, and local customs. They provide valuable insights into the country's history, culture, and practical tips for travelers.

2) **Maps and Navigation Apps:** Carrying a map or using navigation apps like Google Maps or Maps.me can be extremely helpful for getting around in Cambodia, especially in cities and remote areas. They can assist you in finding attractions, navigating public transportation routes, and discovering nearby amenities.

3) **Language Resources:** While English is spoken in tourist areas, having a basic understanding of Khmer, the local language, can greatly enhance your interactions with locals. Language learning apps or

phrasebooks can be useful for learning common greetings, phrases, and essential vocabulary.

4) **Travel Insurance:** It's strongly recommended to have travel insurance that covers medical emergencies, trip cancellations, lost luggage, and other unforeseen circumstances. Ensure that your insurance policy provides adequate coverage for your needs during your stay in Cambodia.

5) **Local SIM Cards and Internet Access:** Purchasing a local SIM card upon arrival in Cambodia allows you to have a reliable and affordable means of communication. Internet access is widely available in major cities and tourist areas, but it may be limited in remote regions.

6) **Local Tourism Offices:** Cambodia has tourism offices in major cities like Phnom Penh and Siem Reap, where you can obtain maps, brochures, and information about local attractions, events, and festivals. The staff can also provide recommendations and assistance with travel arrangements.

7) **Local Transportation Apps:** Ride-hailing apps like Grab and PassApp are popular in Cambodia and can be convenient for booking transportation within cities. They offer a safe and reliable alternative to taxis and tuk-tuks, and the fares are usually pre-determined.

By utilizing these essential travel resources, you can enhance your trip to Cambodia and ensure a more enjoyable and convenient travel experience. Whether it's gathering information, navigating the country, or staying connected, these resources will assist you in making the most of your time in this beautiful and culturally rich destination.

Communication and Internet Access

Staying connected and having reliable communication options while traveling in Cambodia is essential for a smooth and enjoyable trip. Here is an overview of communication and internet access in the country:

1. **Mobile Networks:** Cambodia has a well-developed mobile network infrastructure. Major local mobile operators include Cellcard, Smart Axiata, and Metfone. These providers offer affordable prepaid SIM cards that can be easily purchased at airports, convenience stores, or official stores. Having a local SIM card enables you to make calls, send text messages, and access mobile data.
2. **Internet Access:** Internet access is widely available in Cambodia, particularly in urban areas and tourist destinations. Most hotels, cafes, and restaurants offer free Wi-Fi for guests. In major cities like Phnom Penh and Siem Reap, you'll find internet cafes where you can access the internet for a small fee. However, internet speeds may vary depending on the location and provider.
3. **Data Packages:** Mobile operators in Cambodia offer various data packages that cater to different needs

and budgets. You can choose from daily, weekly, or monthly packages, depending on the duration of your stay. These packages provide you with a certain amount of data for internet browsing, social media usage, and other online activities.

4. **Internet Cafes:** Internet cafes are still available in Cambodia, especially in smaller towns and rural areas. They offer a convenient option for travelers who don't have access to mobile data or need a reliable internet connection for specific tasks like printing documents or conducting online research.
5. **Communication Apps:** Popular communication apps like WhatsApp, Messenger, and Viber work well in Cambodia. These apps allow you to make voice and video calls, send messages, and share media with friends and family over Wi-Fi or mobile data.
6. **Language Barriers:** While English is spoken in many tourist areas, it's helpful to have a translation app or dictionary on your phone for basic communication with locals who may not be fluent in English.

With the availability of mobile networks, Wi-Fi hotspots, and internet cafes, staying connected and accessing the internet in Cambodia is generally convenient. Having a local SIM card and using communication apps will ensure that you can easily connect with others and access important information during your travels in this beautiful country.

Local Customs and Etiquette

When visiting Cambodia, it's important to be aware of the local customs and etiquette to show respect to the culture and people. Here are some key customs and etiquette practices to keep in mind:

1. **Greetings:** The traditional greeting in Cambodia is the "Sampeah," which involves placing your palms together in a prayer-like gesture and slightly bowing your head. This gesture is commonly used to greet others, show respect, and express gratitude. It is polite to return the gesture when someone greets you with a Sampeah.
2. **Modest Dress:** Cambodian culture values modesty, particularly in religious and sacred sites. When visiting temples or pagodas, both men and women should dress conservatively, covering their shoulders and knees. Wearing lightweight, breathable clothing is advisable due to the country's warm climate.
3. **Removing Shoes:** It is customary to remove your shoes before entering someone's home, religious sites, and certain businesses. Look for cues, such as a pile of shoes at the entrance, to determine if you should remove your shoes.

4. **Respecting Monks:** Monks hold a revered position in Cambodian society. If you encounter a monk, show respect by not touching them and refraining from physical contact. When offering donations or receiving blessings, use your right hand or both hands.
5. **Politeness and Courtesy:** Cambodians are generally polite and soft-spoken. Showing respect through polite language, such as using "□□□" (soum) for "please" and "□□□□□" (arkun) for "thank you," is appreciated. Avoid raising your voice or displaying anger in public.
6. **Public Displays of Affection:** Public displays of affection, such as hugging or kissing, are not common in Cambodian culture. It is best to avoid such behavior in public as it may be considered inappropriate or offensive.
7. **Food Etiquette:** When dining in Cambodia, it is customary to wait for the host or the eldest person to begin eating before you start. Use utensils or your right hand to eat, as the left hand is traditionally considered unclean. It is polite to finish all the food on your plate as leaving food may be seen as wasteful.

By respecting and following these customs and etiquette practices, you will create a positive impression, foster meaningful interactions with locals, and show appreciation for Cambodia's rich cultural heritage. Remember, a little cultural sensitivity goes a long way in enhancing your travel experience in this beautiful country.

Safety Tips and Emergency Contacts

Ensuring your safety is essential when traveling to any destination, and Cambodia is no exception. By following these safety tips and being prepared with emergency contacts, you can have a secure and worry-free experience:

1. **Personal Safety:** It's advisable to stay vigilant and aware of your surroundings, especially in crowded areas and tourist spots. Keep an eye on your belongings and be cautious of pickpockets. Avoid displaying expensive items and keep important documents secure.
2. **Transportation Safety:** When using public transportation, choose reputable and licensed operators. Use metered taxis or negotiate fares in advance to avoid overcharging. For tuk-tuks or motorbike taxis, agree on a price before starting the journey. Always wear a helmet if riding a motorbike.
3. **Health and Hygiene:** Carry and drink bottled water to stay hydrated. Avoid consuming uncooked or unpeeled fruits and vegetables, as well as street food with questionable hygiene practices. Use mosquito repellent and take necessary precautions to prevent

mosquito-borne diseases such as dengue fever and malaria.
4. **Cultural Sensitivity:** Respect local customs, traditions, and religious sites. Avoid taking photos without permission, particularly in religious or sacred places. Dress modestly, especially when visiting temples and pagodas.
5. **Emergency Contacts:** Familiarize yourself with the emergency contacts in Cambodia. The general emergency number is 117, which connects you to the police. For medical emergencies, you can call the Cambodian Red Cross Ambulance Service at 119 or visit the nearest hospital.
6. **Embassy or Consulate Contacts:** Make a note of your country's embassy or consulate contact details in Cambodia. They can provide assistance in case of emergencies, such as lost passports, accidents, or legal issues.
7. **Travel Insurance:** Prior to your trip, ensure you have travel insurance that covers medical emergencies, trip cancellation, and other unforeseen circumstances. Keep a copy of your insurance policy and emergency contact information handy.

It's important to stay informed about the current travel advisories for Cambodia and any potential safety concerns. Check the website of your country's embassy or consulate for the latest updates and advice.

Updated Cambodia Travel Guide

By adhering to these safety tips and being prepared with emergency contacts, you can enjoy your time in Cambodia with peace of mind, knowing that you have taken necessary precautions for a safe and memorable journey.

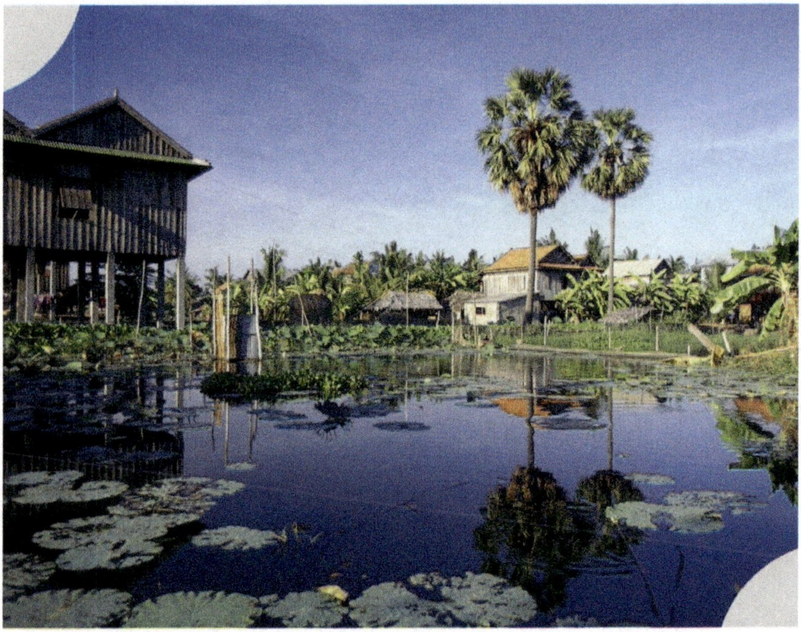

CONCLUSION

The "Updated Cambodia Travel Guide" serves as a comprehensive resource for travelers seeking to explore the captivating beauty and rich cultural heritage of Cambodia. Throughout the pages of this guide, readers will find a wealth of information on various aspects of planning and experiencing a memorable trip to this enchanting country.

From the moment readers dive into the book, they are introduced to an overview of Cambodia, providing insights into its history, geography, and diverse cultural fabric. The guide highlights the unique appeal of Cambodia and the reasons why it should be on every traveler's bucket list.

The guide offers practical information to help readers navigate their way through Cambodia. It covers essential topics such as visa requirements, currency and exchange rates, health and safety tips, transportation options, and more. This ensures that readers are well-prepared and equipped with the necessary knowledge to make their journey smooth and enjoyable.

The book provides detailed sections on popular destinations like Phnom Penh, Siem Reap, and the coastal and island getaways, offering a comprehensive exploration of each location. Readers can discover top attractions, dining and nightlife options, shopping experiences, accommodation choices, and insider tips to make the most of their time in each destination.

Additionally, the guide delves into the renowned Angkor Archaeological Park, unraveling the mystique of the ancient temples, providing valuable insights into exploring the park, and offering tips to enhance the overall experience. It also explores other regions of Cambodia, such as Battambang, Kampong Cham, and the countryside, providing readers with a well-rounded understanding of the country's diverse landscapes and cultural heritage.

Throughout the guide, emphasis is placed on cultural sensitivity, local customs, and responsible travel practices, ensuring that readers can engage respectfully with the local communities and leave a positive impact.

The "Updated Cambodia Travel Guide" is more than just a collection of information; it is a companion that inspires readers to embark on a journey of discovery, immersing themselves in Cambodia's vibrant history, breathtaking landscapes, and warm hospitality. It encourages readers to step out of their comfort zones, explore hidden gems, and create unforgettable memories.

Updated Cambodia Travel Guide

In closing, the "Updated Cambodia Travel Guide" serves as an indispensable tool for travelers seeking an authentic and enriching experience in Cambodia. It equips readers with the knowledge, tips, and insights to navigate the country with confidence, immerse themselves in its beauty, and create lifelong memories. Whether it's exploring ancient temples, interacting with locals, or indulging in the local cuisine, this guide empowers readers to embark on an unforgettable adventure in the Kingdom of Wonder.

Can You Do Me A Favor?

Are you one of the thousands of people who have read my book on Updated Cambodia Travel Guide? If so, I'd love to hear your thoughts! Please take a few moments to drop a review on Amazon and let me know what you think. Your opinion matters, and I'm sure your review will help others decide if this book is right for them. Thank you so much for being a part of this journey.

With sincere gratitude,

Emily Michaels.

Printed in Great Britain
by Amazon